SAINTUARIE

A Journey for Intentional Holiness

Editing, Design and Photographs by
ANTHONY THAXTON

Christ Church Director of Communications
JO ELLEN DRUELINGER

CC Global Executive Director
MAXIE DUNNAM

Ministry Coordinator of CC Global
NATHAN BRASFIELD

www.cumcmemphis.org

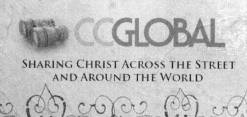

SHARING CHRIST ACROSS THE STREET
AND AROUND THE WORLD

40 DAY READING AND PRAYER GUIDE FOR THE LENTEN SEASON

SAINTUARIE

A Journey for Intentional Holiness

Shane Stanford and Pokey Stanford

CCGLOBAL

ACKNOWLEDGEMENTS

Thank you to our
Christ Church family
and staff for continuing
to reach for the best of all
God has in store.

Be Salt and Light . . .
You matter!

Shane Stanford and Pokey Stanford

For
MAXIE DUNNAM

*It is a joy to serve with you
in this place you've prepared*

Shane Stanford and Pokey Stanford

INTRODUCTION

What is Saintuarie?

The word 'Saintuarie' literally means 'a life of intentional holiness'. Much like a 'Sanctuary'—which is a place of intentional holiness—Saintuarie becomes the living expression of God's work and plan for life. The definition marks the journey by its own expressions—life, intentional, holy.
The following reading plan focuses on each of these means for drawing close to the God who has already drawn close to you.

If Lent is a season of personal spiritual formation; then Saintuarie is the life that, literally, takes spiritual formation personally.

How to use the guide?

The *Saintuarie 40-Day Lenten Reading Guide* prepares the reader for the journey from Ash Wednesday through Easter. To maximize the use of the guide, do the following:

1. Read the Scripture. You will want to look up the entire passage as well as read the printed Scripture.
2. Prepare your heart for the day by saying the prayer.
3. Use the "Life Questions" to focus your journal references and entries.
4. Attend worship services available for a more complete connection to the Easter Story and miracle of the Cross and Resurrection.
5. Join a Lenten Bible Study Group. This year's theme is *The Intercessory Life* by Maxie Dunnam.

ASH WEDNESDAY

Reflect

"Taste and see that the Lord is good". Take time to reflect
on the love and grace of God. Our journey to holiness begins
by looking briefly to the broken places and fractures of our
past, not that we remain there, but so that we establish a clear
path for where (and where not) to not tread in the future.

DAY ONE

Reflect

ASH WEDNESDAY
Scripture: Matthew 6:21

*Wherever your treasure is,
there the desires of your heart will also be.*

Prayer: Gracious God, we are thankful for your grace and for your forgiveness when we run everywhere, in every direction BUT to You. Heal our hearts, redirect our paths, engage our souls to want better, desire more and to seek for the treasure that is Your love. We pray in Jesus. Amen.

Life Question: Name your "treasures"? What makes them valuable to you? Are they worth the effort? Do your desires for them draw you closer to God, or push you down an unhealthy path away from Him?

DAY TWO

Reflect

Scripture: Judges 2:10-15

Every time Israel went out to battle, the Lord fought against them, causing them to be defeated, just as he had warned. And the people were in great distress.

Prayer: Gracious God, we are tired of running, of making the next step, the next issue about ourselves instead of looking to you. We want more from life. We know that you have more in store. Father, we pray that you will rescue us from the distress of our rebellion, in whatever forms it lives in us. Give us your heart, your direction at this crossroads of our lives. You believe in us. Help us to believe in ourselves. We pray in Jesus. Amen.

Life Question: In what ways are you in "distress" today? How do these broken places keep you from seeing God's will for your life? How do they keep you from choosing God's new direction?

DAY THREE

Reflect

Scripture: Ezekiel 20:13-20

I am the LORD your God; follow my decrees and be careful to keep my laws. Keep my Sabbaths holy, that they may be a sign between us. Then you will know that I am the LORD your God."

Prayer: Gracious God, we thank you for a love that doesn't make sense. We praise you for grace that doesn't seem possible. We love you for a new beginning that doesn't come fast enough. We know now… about our sin, about your grace, about our pain, about your love… that you are OUR God. In Jesus. Amen.

Life Questions: In what ways, do you "remember" God's promise for grace and forgiveness in your life? How do your actions and decisions point to God's place in your journey? In what ways, do others see the "hands and feet of Jesus" in your world?

DAY FOUR

Reflect

Scripture: Jeremiah 3:19-22

"I thought to myself, 'I would love to treat you as my own children!' I wanted nothing more than to give you this beautiful land—the finest possession in the world. I looked forward to your calling me 'Father,'and I wanted you never to turn from me.

Prayer: Gracious God, we are most hesitant to fly than you are to catch us. You continue to plead with us, "Do not be afraid…" Why can't we accept Your promises? Give us courage to be still, and to trust that you will catch us… We spend so much time, dear God, being so little, in spite of you giving us so much. We love you. Be patient with us. In Jesus. Amen.

Life Questions: What weights in life keep you grounded? How does God call you to "leap forward" today? In what ways are we afraid to "fly" into His presence and become all that He has in store?

FIRST SUNDAY

Rest

Scripture: Matthew 11: 28-30

"Then Jesus said, "Come to me, all of you who are weary and carry heavy burdens, and I will give you rest. Take my yoke upon you. Let me teach you, because I am humble and gentle at heart, and you will find rest for your souls. For my yoke is easy to bear, and the burden I give you is light."

Our journey for intentional holiness requires strength and clarity of body, mind and soul. As with any 'quest', the healthier the pilgrim, the greater chance for success. As one of the world's great spiritual teachers would ask of his students, "So, how is it with your soul?"

DAY FIVE

Rest

Scripture: Numbers 20:1-13

Why did you make us leave Egypt and bring us here to this terrible place? This land has no grain, no figs, no grapes, no pomegranates, and no water to drink!"

Prayer: Gracious God, we thank you for speaking into our souls with such sweet words and grace. You are loud enough to be heard, and soft enough in your words to be understood. We thank you for your patience. We want to "get it right" the first time. We want to step into the promise of what You have so beautifully prepared for us. We love you. In Jesus. Amen.

Life Questions: What is the noise in your life today? How does the noise keep you from hearing and understanding God's plan for your life? How can you lower the volume to hear what God is saying?

DAY SIX

Rest

Scripture: Ecclesiastes 12:13-14

That's the whole story. Here now is my final conclusion:
Fear God and obey his commands, for this is everyone's duty.
God will judge us for everything we do, including every
secret thing, whether good or bad.

Prayer: Gracious God, we love you for taking away our burdens. We praise you for ripping them from our hands at times. We are grateful that 'most' is not good enough when it comes to 'how much' of us you desire. We are yours. You are ours. We are blessed. We love you. In Jesus. Amen.

Life Questions: What burdens do you struggle to put down today? In what ways does God call for you to rest in his care, only to have you bear the baggage anyway? How would "resting in Christ" change the trajectory of your faith?

DAY SEVEN

Rest

Scripture: Romans 5:1-2

Therefore, since we have been made right in God's sight by faith, we have peace with God because of what Jesus Christ our Lord has done for us. Because of our faith, Christ has brought us into this place of undeserved privilege where we now stand, and we confidently and joyfully look forward to sharing God's glory.

Prayer: Gracious God, thank you for providing so much for us. But, also, thank you for expecting so much from us. We are not only called to experience the joy and confidence of You in our lives, but to live that promise to the world, so that through us, others will see You. What a blessing! We love you. In Jesus. Amen.

Life Questions: What are the elements of your journey that are working right? What are the elements that are not working right? Are you at peace with God? How does that feel? Are you unsettled? If so, why? How has this disconnection affected your journey?

DAY EIGHT

Rest

Scripture: Ephesians 2:14-18

*For Christ himself has brought peace to us. He united Jews
and Gentiles into one people when, in his own body on the
cross, he broke down the wall of hostility that separated us.*

Prayer: Gracious God, we thank you for our blessings, and
especially for the basic necessities that allow for our bodies
to be whole. Fill our souls just the same. We hunger and
thirst of you… you become our fill and our sufficiency. We
love you, Dear Father. In Jesus. Amen.

Life Questions: What do you hunger for in your life today?
What keeps you up at night, weeping, broken or worried?
What do you need to fill the inner places of our your soul that
you are never empty and never alone?

DAY NINE

Rest

Scripture: Mark 8:11-13

The Pharisees came and began to question Jesus. To test him, they asked him for a sign from heaven. He sighed deeply and said, "Why does this generation ask for a sign? Truly I tell you, no sign will be given to it." Then he left them, got back into the boat and crossed to the other side.

Prayer: Gracious God, we pray for quiet in soul. We pray for patience to hear what You are saying to us. We pray for courage to truly listen. We pray for wisdom to follow. Father, we are so much less than what you deserve, and, yet, though your Son, you have made us so much more than what the world deserves. Thank you for that. We are blessed. We love you. In Jesus. Amen.

Life Questions: What are the questions that cause you to be restless today? What restless places prick at your soul until the blood drains your strength? What makes for the strongest and best parts of who we are called to be. What places, people and purpose areas sing the praise of your triumph? What of those same places, people and purpose that do more harm than good no matter how hard we try? You are not a facsimile of yourself. You are the real deal. Do you live like it?

DAY TEN

Rest

Scripture: Philippians 4:6-7

*Do not be anxious about anything, but in every situation,
by prayer and petition, with thanksgiving, present
your requests to God. And the peace of God, which
transcends all understanding, will guard your hearts
and your minds in Christ Jesus.*

Prayer: Gracious God, we thank you for being so willing to hear our prayers and celebrate our blessings. What would we do without you! Give us wisdom to follow your example, and to trust your will. We love you. In Jesus. Amen.

Life Questions: What makes you anxious today? How do those anxieties affect your life? Make a list of those concerns that hold you back from God. Now, make a list of those celebrations and blessings in your life. What are your requests for both lists? Present your requests to God with 'petitions' and 'thanksgiving'.

SECOND SUNDAY

Restore

Have mercy on me, O God, because of your unfailing love. Because of your great compassion, blot out the stain of my sins Wash me clean from my guilt. Purify me from my sin.

Psalm 51: 1-15

Our journey for intentional holiness means first restoring the broken edges of our spiritual journey and relationships. Where are the places in your life, where restoration must occur. Take time to pray for healing and hope to erupt in your daily life.

DAY ELEVEN

Restore

Scripture: Matthew 27: 3-10

When Judas, who had betrayed him, realized that Jesus had been condemned to die, he was filled with remorse. So he took the thirty pieces of silver back to the leading priests and the elders. "I have sinned," he declared, "for I have betrayed an innocent man." "What do we care?" they retorted. "That's your problem."

Prayer: Gracious God, Remind us daily of your sacrifice, and keep us from the selfish ways that betray your love for us again and again. We are sorry for how we fail you. Give us presence of mind to recognize our weakness and live out your grace. We love you. In Jesus. Amen.

Life Questions: In what ways have you betrayed the best parts of your life? Maybe it is a relationship, a responsibility or the use of a resource. How have you betrayed God? How do the regrets of our mistakes define and control us? What keeps us from accepting God's unconditional love for past mistakes? How could this acceptance change our circumstances?

DAY TWELVE

Restore

Scripture: 2 Samuel 12: 1-23

Then Nathan said to David, "You are that man! The Lord, the God of Israel, says: I anointed you king of Israel and saved you from the power of Saul. I gave you your master's house and his wives and the kingdoms of Israel and Judah. And if that had not been enough, I would have given you much, much more.

Prayer: Gracious God, we are humbled by our weaknesses and transformed by your grace. Give us courage to accept your forgiveness and wisdom to follow your path of restoration for our lives. We want to live different, Dear Father. We want to live in you. We love you. In Jesus. Amen.

Life Questions: Have you ever had your mistakes pointed out to you? How did that make you feel? What good comes from facing our mistakes? How do the lessons reveal a better opportunity for us? What broken places remain hidden in you? How can you confront those today?

DAY THIRTEEN

Restore

Scripture: 2 Corinthians 7: 10

For the kind of sorrow God wants us to experience leads us away from sin and results in salvation. There's no regret for that kind of sorrow. But worldly sorrow, which lacks repentance, results in spiritual death.

Prayer: Gracious God, we are humbled by your deep love for us. Your lessons for our lives seem so difficult to the world, but we know that you use even our weakest places to shape our hearts and lives. Thank you for not giving up on us. Protect us from the broken intentions of this world and give us strength to go forward in your name.

Life Questions: Are you moving past your regret? Have you truly accepted God's love and grace to a new depth that cleanses all past sins? What help are you seeking from Godly friends that move you into His new future? Are there any patterns that may be keeping you in your past that you need to change?

DAY FOURT

Restor

Scripture: Ezekiel 6: 8-

*"But I will let a few of my people escape destru
scattered among the nations of the world. The
among the nations, they will remember me.
how hurt I am by their unfaithful hearts and
for their idols. Then at last they will hate the
detestable sins. They will know that I alone ar
was serious when I said I would bring this cala
is what the Sovereign Lord says: Clap your h
stamp your feet. Cry out because of all the dete
of Israel have committed. Now they are g
war and famine and diseas*

Prayer: Gracious God, forgive my dependence
all too often seek the world's approval rather tha
and forgiveness are so abundant, yet often I will
full acceptance of you. Grant me the strength to
align my heart to Yours. In your precious Son's r

Life Questions: What are the idols of this world th
that keep me in a season of regret? How am I keep
from the alignment of His will? How can I seek His
specific way?

DAY FIFTEEN

Restore

Scripture: John 9:35-41

When Jesus heard what had happened, he found the man and asked, "Do you believe in the Son of Man?t" The man answered, "Who is he, sir? I want to believe in him." "You have seen him," Jesus said, "and he is speaking to you!" "Yes, Lord, I believe!" the man said. And he worshiped Jesus. Then Jesus told him, "I entered this world to render judgment—to give sight to the blind and to show those who think they see that they are blind." Some Pharisees who were standing nearby heard him and asked, "Are you saying we're blind?" "If you were blind, you wouldn't be guilty," Jesus replied. "But you remain guilty because you claim you can see.

Prayer: Sovereign Lord, our healer and redeemer, Help us to believe and seek to dispel our regretful disbelief that binds us to the flesh. Lord, open our eyes that we may see only your will and Your ways and will let go of the past unbelief.

Life Questions: In what ways are you holding on to past unbelief? Do you truly believe that God can heal? Is there any part of your past that you have been "blind" to that He now helps you see clearly? How will acknowledging this help move you past unbelief to a newfound and unwavering trust in our Lord?

DAY SIXTEEN

Restore

Scripture: Psalm 54:1-3

Come with great power, O God, and rescue me! Defend me with your might. Listen to my prayer, O God. Pay attention to my plea. For strangers are attacking me; violent people are trying to kill me. They care nothing for God.

Prayer: Gracious God, our prayers, oftentimes, become too much about us and not enough about You. Sometimes, I feel like the world is against me, but I realize that most of my problems come from my own failures and missteps. Help me to be gracious and forgiving, as You have been with me. Putting the focus on someone else is not solving my problems. Help me focus on my issues first and trust that You are sufficient in all things. We love you, Father. In Jesus. Amen.

Life Questions: What are the issues that cause you to blame others (even God) instead of putting the real focus on yourself? What happens when you confront your weakest parts and problems? How would you feel if others put the blame on you for their issues? Make a list of "Responsibility Requests"—Frame them in "Today, I will take responsibility for..." Keep a journal of how God begins to work in these requests.

Reac

Scripture: Isaiah 5

*But it was the Lord's good plan to cri
grief.   Yet when his life is made an
have many descendants.   He will er
Lord's good plan will prospe
Isaiah 53: 10*

Our journey for intentional holiness er
for God's 'new beginnings' in life. A p
important things, people, and places.
for in life?

DAY SEVENTEEN

Reach

Scripture: 1 Peter 5: 7

*Give all your worries and cares to God,
for he cares about you.*

Prayer: Gracious God, Our Hope and Redeemer. But, Father, you are more ready to hear us than we are often ready to pray. Thank you for your patience and for Your promise to never leave or forsake us. We know that your love and care for us is greater than any issue this world or the Adversary can throw our way. Give us strength to face our struggles, and wisdom to let go our need to face them alone. We love you. In Jesus. Amen.

Life Questions: What are your worries? How do they affect your daily life? How do they affect your walk with God? What does it mean to 'give' your cares and worries away? What would look different in your life if you did this? What is stopping you from doing so?

DAY EIGHTEEN

Reach

Scripture: John 14: 15-26

*"If you love me, obey my commandments.
And I will ask the Father, and he will give you another
Advocate, who will never leave you.*

Prayer: Gracious God, our Peace, our Hope, our Friend.
Give us wisdom to follow your commandments. You have
given them to us for our own good, to protect and to guide.
And, thank you for the gift of your Holy Spirit, who speaks
and intercedes for us in the best and worst of times. Father,
we know the world can be difficult. You told your disciples
this very truth. But, you also promised that you have
'overcome the world'. We cling to this promise, knowing we
are never alone—never abandoned. We love you. In Jesus.
Amen.

Life Questions: What are the easiest commandments for you
to keep? What are the most difficult? What keeps us from
living out the commandments on a regular basis? What is
your opinion of the Holy Spirit? Why did God the Father and
God the Son send us the Holy Spirit? Do you ever feel alone?
On your own on this journey? What would it mean to know
the God is always with you?

DAY NINETEEN

Reach

Scripture: Romans 8: 38

And I am convinced that nothing can ever separate us from God's love. Neither death nor life, neither angels nor demons, neither our fears for today nor our worries about tomorrow— not even the powers of hell can separate us from God's love.

Prayer: Gracious God, our Strength and Shield. We thank you for standing in the gap for us, and for assuring us that nothing can separate us from Your love. Father, we fear so much in our lives. No matter how 'strong' we are, each of us has something that breaks down the defenses. But, you are unafraid. We thank you for your grace and for your patience. Help us to not only know of your promise, but to live as those who claim it and cling to it. The world needs to see a difference. The world needs this hope. Thank you for being so much more than we can imagine. We love you. In Jesus. Amen.

Life Questions: What keeps you up at night? What fears are bigger than you are, even if you don't admit it to others? What are the 'powers of hell' in your journey? What does 'nothing' mean to you? How does God's promise that 'nothing' can separate us affect the ways we approach God, the world, each other and our struggles?

DAY TWENTY

Reach

Scripture: John 6: 37

*However, those the Father has given me will come
to me, and I will never reject them.*

Prayer: Gracious God, thank you for loving us so much.
Your care for us is beyond question and we have nothing to
fear. You have accepted us as we are, and you want the best
for us. The gift of your Son, Jesus, is more than we deserve
and more than we can imagine. We are grateful. Help us to
be faithful. We love you. In Jesus. Amen.

Life Questions: What does it mean for God to meet us
where we are? How does such acceptance affect you? Your
understanding of God? Your understanding of others? What
does such acceptance mean for your service to the world?

DAY TWENTY-ONE

Reach

Scripture: Hebrews 13:5

Keep your lives free from the love of money and be content with what you have, because God has said, "Never will I leave you; never will I forsake you."

Prayer: Gracious God, we so often become entangled by the things of this world. And, the farther we are from you, the more entangled we are. Help us to not make other gods of the things of this world. But, help us to keep our eyes on you. You promise to never leave us, give us hope, a new day and place as your children. What more could we ask? We belong to you. We love you. In Jesus. Amen.

Life Questions: How do the things of this world, like money, affect the way we see God? What do our contentment and God's plan for our lives have in common? How does discontentment lead us away from God? What does it mean that God 'never leaves us, and never forsakes us'?

DAY TWENTY-TWO

Reach

Scripture: John 8:1-11

*Then Jesus stood up again and said to the woman,
"Where are your accusers? Didn't even one of them
condemn you?" "No, Lord," she said. And Jesus
said, "Neither do I. Go and sin no more."*

Prayer: Gracious God, we thank you for bending into the dirt with us. You write your message on our hearts, and we are not the same. Help us to find your forgiveness, to take hold of your grace and to live a life worthy of your love. Thank you for making us more than we could ever become on our own. We love you. In Jesus. Amen.

Life Questions: What does it mean for Jesus to write in the dirt? Why would he be 'stalling'? What does Jesus want the crowd to understand? What does he want the woman to see? How can God's justice mix with God's love? What does it mean for Jesus to send our accusers away? What does it mean for us to 'go and sin no more'?

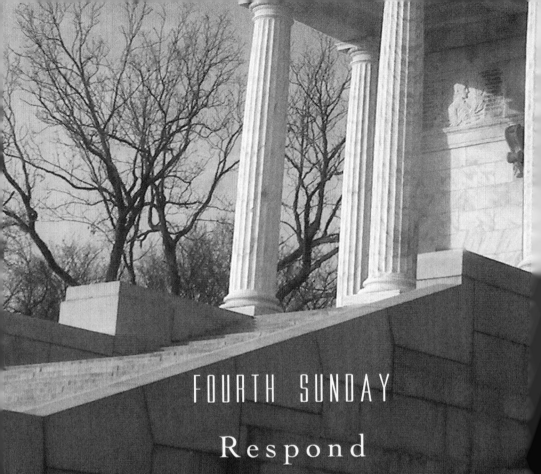

FOURTH SUNDAY

Respond

Our journey for intentional holiness requires opportunities for answering God's call upon our life beyond our encounter of God in prayer and study. God also calls us to 'make a difference' in our world—to 'respond' as the 'hands and feet of Jesus'. How are you 'responding' to God's call in your world, in this season of your life?

Genesis 3:12-13

The Lord had said to Abram, "Leave your native country, your relatives, and your father's family, and go to the land that I will show you. I will make you into a great nation. I will bless you and make you famous, and you will be a blessing to others. I will bless those who bless you and curse those who treat you with contempt. All the families on earth will be blessed through you."

So Abram departed as the Lord had instructed, and Lot went with him. Abram was seventy-five years old when he left Haran.

DAY TWENTY-THREE

Respond

Scripture: Matthew 27:15-26

Pilate saw that he wasn't getting anywhere and that a riot was developing. So he sent for a bowl of water and washed his hands before the crowd, saying, "I am innocent of the blood of this man. The responsibility is yours!" And all the people yelled back, "We will take responsibility for his death -- we and our children!" So Pilate released Barabbas to them. He ordered Jesus flogged with a lead-tipped whip, then turned him over to the Roman soldiers to crucify him.

Prayer: Gracious God, you place in my heart what is good and right and just. Help me to honor those things and speak those things when the court of public opinion and peer pressure would have me do otherwise. Make me brave enough to throw aside the shield of silence when I see injustice. As I depend on your grace for all that I am and all that I do, let me show that same grace to all that I meet. In Jesus. Amen.

Life Questions: Have you ever seen someone being mistreated and walked silently away? Have you ever sat through a contentious discussion in a meeting without speaking your heart, excusing yourself because you "believe" what is right? How many times do we mentally "wash our hands" of the injustice of the world because we know our own heart?

DAY TWENTY-FOUR

Respond

Scripture: Numbers 1:50-51

Put the Levites in charge of the Tabernacle of the Covenant, along with all its furnishings and equipment. They must carry the Tabernacle and all its furnishings as you travel, and they must take care of it and camp around it. Whenever it is time for the Tabernacle to move, the Levites will take it down. And when it is time to stop, they will set it up again...

Prayer: Gracious God, we take seriously the tasks that you have given us. We are often faint of heart and easily distracted, but you never fail to "show up" when we need you. We love and appreciate the way you speak into our circumstances and make each day full of possibilities. Thank you for making our journey mean something more than we can imagine. We love you. In Jesus. Amen.

Life Questions: What has God called you to do in order that his glory might show? What is the most difficult job God has given you? Why was it so difficult? Describe the way you responded to the last request God made of your life and time. How did that response shape the job you did? What can the world learn from our faithfulness to do our best for God?

DAY TWENTY-FIVE

Respond

Scripture: Galatians 6:7-8

Don't be misled—you cannot mock the justice of God. You will always harvest what you plant. Those who live only to satisfy their own sinful nature will harvest decay and death from that sinful nature. But those who live to please the Spirit will harvest everlasting life from the Spirit.

Prayer: Gracious God, we thank you for connecting us to your love in such specific ways. We appreciate the ways you push us out of our comfort zones and make us your own. We are not the same when we have been in your presence, and neither are those for whom you have called us to respond. That responsibility bears fruit that lasts forever. What a privilege! We love you. In Jesus. Amen.

Life Questions: What does it mean to 'please the Spirit'? What about 'harvest everlasting life'? What does it look like 'when a dream dies'? Why do dreams 'die' so hard? What happens when a 'dream is born'? Contrast the last two questions.

DAY TWENTY-SIX

Respond

Scripture: Romans 12:6-8

In his grace, God has given us different gifts for doing certain things well. So if God has given you the ability to prophesy, speak out with as much faith as God has given you. If your gift is serving others, serve them well. If you are a teacher, teach well. If your gift is to encourage others, be encouraging. If it is giving, give generously. If God has given you leadership ability, take the responsibility seriously. And if you have a gift for showing kindness to others, do it gladly.

Prayer: God of Faithfulness, you are more ready to hear our prayers than we are to pray them. You call us to serve you and to serve each other. Give us strength and wisdom to use the gifts you have given us to be the best for your will. Help us to live out our passion area and to make the most of sharing your Word. Make us more like you, Father. We love you. In Jesus. Amen.

Life Questions: Make a list of your gifts. What are the skills and gifts you believe God has asked you to carry for him? What are your passion areas for ministry? How can God use your gifts to make a difference for his will in the world?

DAY TWENTY-SEVEN

Respond

Scripture: 1 John 4:7-17

Dear friends, let us continue to love one another, for love comes from God. Anyone who loves is a child of God and knows God. But anyone who does not love does not know God, for God is love.

Prayer: Oh Great God, thank you for your unfailing and unwavering love. The gift of your only Son teaches me that your love for us is deeper than anything we can understand. Help me accept your love and then reach out to share it with others. Thank you for the gift of love in Jesus. Amen.

Life Questions: How am I sharing the love of Christ in my daily walk? In what ways can I be more like Christ in showing love? What does it truly mean to love my brothers and sisters like Christ?

DAY TWENTY-EIGHT

Respond

Scripture: Matthew 25: 29

*To those who use well what they are given, even
more will be given, and they will have an abundance.
But from those who do nothing, even what little
they have will be taken away.*

Prayer: Dear God, teach me to use the gifts you have given
me to bring you glory. Open my eyes where there are
opportunities that I am not able to see and open my ears to
hear your calling today. Amen.

Life Questions: What spiritual gifts has God given me that I've
yet to use? What keeps me from using the gifts he has given
me? How can I seek to use my gifts in my church, home and
community?

FIFTH SUNDAY

Replenish

Scripture: Malachi 3:10

Bring all the tithes into the storehouse so there will be enough food in my Temple. If you do," says the Lord of Heaven's Armies, "I will open the windows of heaven for you. I will pour out a blessing so great you won't have enough room to take it in! Try it!
Put me to the test!"

Our journey for intentional holiness is a journey for a reason, meaning that we must begin, pause and begin again in the process of faithfully seeking God. What are the ways you 'replenish' both your personal spiritual gifts and the hope and joy for your journey?

Replenish

Scripture: John 3:16-17

"For God loved the world so much that he gave his one and only Son, so that everyone who believes in him will not perish but have eternal life. God sent his Son into the world not to judge the world, but to save the world through him.

Prayer: Gracious Lord, you gave it all for us in the gift of Jesus. Teach me today to share that gift with those whom I come in contact. With a grateful heart. Amen.

Life Question: What am I willing to give for the word?

DAY THIRTY

Replenish

Scripture: Luke 21: 1-4

While Jesus was in the Temple, he watched the rich people dropping their gifts in the collection box. Then a poor widow came by and dropped in two small coins. "I tell you the truth," Jesus said, "this poor widow has given more than all the rest of them. For they have given a tiny part of their surplus, but she, poor as she is, has given everything she has."

Prayer: God of Wonders, teach me to give out of my poverty, not out of my abundance. Help me to understand that you will provide my needs and that it is only when I give my all that you can fill me up with what I truly need. Today, help me to put more of you in my heart and less of my earthly desires. Amen.

Life Questions: Do I give out of abundance or out of poverty? Where do I need to give more? How do I find the courage to give until I am empty?

DAY THIRTY-ONE

Replenish

Scripture: Psalm 54:6

I will sacrifice a voluntary offering to you;
I will praise your name, O Lord, for it is good.
For you have rescued me from my troubles and
helped me to triumph over my enemies.

Prayer: Lord, you are good and worthy of our praise. You continue to bring me out of troubled times and trying days. Help me to continue to focus on you as my source of strength and energy and life and nothing else. Use all of me today, God. Thank you for the gift of today. Amen.

Life Questions: How has God carried me out of troubled times? How will I sacrifice for him? Have I ever been in a circumstance that seemed impossible, yet over time God worked it out? Have I thanked him for his solutions?

DAY THIRTY-TWO

Replenish

Scripture: 2 Corinthians 9:10-11

For God is the one who provides seed for the farmer and then bread to eat. In the same way, he will provide and increase your resources and then produce a great harvest of generosity in you. Yes, you will be enriched in every way so that you can always be generous. And when we take your gifts to those who need them, they will thank God.

Prayer: God, thank you for always providing my needs. Use today to teach me that I want for much more than I truly need. Help me to see that all I truly need is you. In your precious Son's name, our Savior, Jesus. Amen.

Life Questions: In what ways do I live in abundance and take it for granted? Do I really understand that ALL that I have comes from God? Is there anything that I can share today with those who are in need?

DAY THIRTY-THREE

Replenish

Scripture: 1 Peter 4:10

God has given each of you a gift from his great variety of spiritual gifts. Use them well to serve one another.

Prayer: Creator of All, open my heart and eyes to the power of your Holy Spirit that I will clearly see the spiritual gifts you have given me. Make me aware of how to use these gifts to glorify you. Amen.

Life Questions: What are my spiritual gifts? Would those close to me know that I have spiritual gifts? How do I use them? Are there missed opportunities to use my gifts?

DAY THIRTY-FOUR

Replenish

Scripture: Proverbs 3: 9-10

Honor the Lord with your wealth and with the best part of everything you produce. Then he will fill your barns with grain, and your vats will overflow with good wine.

Prayer: Lord, help me to give you the first fruits of my labor, not just the leftovers. Break my heart to be in line with your heart so that I can fully become all that you intend for me to be. With gratitude. Amen.

Life Questions: Do I give God the first of my money, time and energy? Does he get the leftovers of my money, time and energy? How can he become my priority for every day, not just another obligation?

SIXTH SUNDAY

Recreate

Scripture: 1 Samuel 18:1-4

After David had finished talking with Saul, he met Jonathan,
the king's son. There was an immediate bond between them, for
Jonathan loved David. From that day on Saul kept David with
him and wouldn't let him return home. And Jonathan made
a solemn pact with David, because he loved him as he loved
himself. Jonathan sealed the pact by taking off his robe and
giving it to David, together with his tunic, sword, bow, and belt.

**Our journey for intentional holiness works back to our
intended 'beginning' in Christ. As with Fitzgerald's** *Curious
Case of Benjamin Button***, our journey leads us back to our
'beginning'—God's intended plan for all of us from the
start of Creation. Our goal is to 're-create' the full
'Image of God' in each of our lives**

DAY THIRTY-FIVE

Recreate

Scripture: Genesis 50:14-21

*But Joseph replied, "Don't be afraid of me. Am I God,
that I can punish you? You intended to harm me, but God
intended it all for good. He brought me to this position so I could
save the lives of many people. No, don't be afraid. I will continue
to take care of you and your children." So he reassured
them by speaking kindly to them.*

Prayer: Thank you, God, that you can work out all of my
human errors. Thank you that you are a God of grace and
forgiveness and second chances. Thank you for loving me
and seeking a relationship with me. God, please make me
more like you today. Amen.

Life Questions: Are there any relationships that I need to
repair? Is there forgiveness that I need to either seek or give to
heal a broken relationship?

DAY THIRTY-SIX

Recreate

Scripture: John 5:7

"I can't, sir," the sick man said, "for I have no one to put me into the pool when the water bubbles up. Someone else always gets there ahead of me."

Prayer: God of all healing, make me aware of those I need to help and open my eyes to the areas that I need to seek help. Thank you for providing Godly friends to me and make me the kind of friend that I need to be. Amen.

Life Questions: Am I a good friend? What do I need to do to become a better friend? How can I adjust my sight to look for the needs of others? What distractions can I remove that are hindering me to truly be someone's brother or sister?

DAY THIRTY-SEVEN

Recreate

Scripture: Ephesians 4:32

Instead, be kind to each other, tenderhearted, forgiving one another, just as God through Christ has forgiven you.

Prayer: Thank you for forgiveness. Thank you for loving me. Thank you for the gift of your one and only Son. Amen.

Life Questions: Have I forgiven others the same way that Christ forgave me? What keeps me from forgiving? How can I be more forgiving? Is there someone I need to call today and ask them to forgive me?

DAY THIRTY-EIGHT

Recreate

Scripture: Luke 22: 7-20

He took some bread and gave thanks to God for it.
Then he broke it in pieces and gave it to the disciples, saying,
"This is my body, which is given for you. Do this to remember
me." After supper he took another cup of wine and said,
"This cup is the new covenant between God and his people—
an agreement confirmed with my blood, which is poured
out as a sacrifice for you."

Prayer: God of Goodness, thank you for meeting us at The Table and calling us family. We have wandered so much and for so long that we forgot we belonged to a King. Your love is beyond compare. You taught us to serve and to share. But, more than anything, you reminded us of why we give thanks each day. You broke the bread, now break our hearts. Make us into your image, and give us away to a hungry world. We love you. In Jesus. Amen.

Life Questions: What is your picture of God? Is he angry with you? Disappointed? Aloof? What does a God who meets you at the table look like? What does it mean to be at the same table with someone? What does it mean to share bread? Fellowship? What does it mean to have the host become the servant by washing your feet? Take a moment to breathe it in. Feel anything? If so, what?

DAY THIRTY-NINE

Recreate

Scripture: Matthew 27: 32-61

Along the way, they came across a man named Simon, who was from Cyrene, and the soldiers forced him to carry Jesus' cross. And they went out to a place called Golgotha (which means "Place of the Skull"). The soldiers gave him wine mixed with bitter gall, but when he had tasted it, he refused to drink it.

After they had nailed him to the cross, the soldiers gambled for his clothes by throwing dice. Then they sat around and kept guard as he hung there. A sign was fastened to the cross above Jesus' head, announcing the charge against him. It read: "This is Jesus, the King of the Jews." Two revolutionaries were crucified with him, one on his right and one on his left.

The people passing by shouted abuse, shaking their heads in mockery. "Look at you now!" they yelled at him. "You said you were going to destroy the Temple and rebuild it in three days. Well then, if you are the Son of God, save yourself and come down from the cross!" The leading priests, the teachers of religious law, and the elders also mocked Jesus.

"He saved others," they scoffed, "but he can't save himself! So he is the King of Israel, is he? Let him come down from the cross right now, and we will believe in him! He trusted God, so let

God rescue him now if he wants him! For he said,
'I am the Son of God.'" Even the revolutionaries who were
crucified with him ridiculed him in the same way.

Prayer: God of Good Friday and God of the Cross, it is
hard for me to read this without feeling ashamed. Maybe I
should. But, you have said we were not left at the Cross. We
are resurrection people. But, sometimes, it feels A LOT like
Black Friday in my life. Give me hope, Father. Help me to
see you, even when the world has done a great job of hiding
your face from me. I need remarkable. I need profound.
I need unbelievable. I need you. In Jesus. Amen.

Life Questions: Have you ever watched anyone die? What
were the feelings? Why does death scare us so much? Have
you ever watched a capital punishment? What about the death
of an innocent man? How does that make us feel? How would
we feel if we knew that we were the cause? Why is it easier to
scoff at others and their situations than to stand in the gap for
justice, peace and joy?

Shane Stanford and Pokey Stanford

Recreate

Holy Saturday

Scripture: Matthew 27:62-66

*The next day, on the Sabbath, the leading priests
and Pharisees went to see Pilate. They told him, "Sir, we
remember what that deceiver once said while he was
still alive: 'After three days I will rise from the dead.'*

*So we request that you seal the tomb until the third day.
This will prevent his disciples from coming and stealing
his body and then telling everyone he was raised
from the dead! If that happens, we'll be worse off
than we were at first."*

*Pilate replied, "Take guards and secure it
the best you can." So they sealed the tomb and
posted guards to protect it.*

Prayer:

God of the empty grave. Friday was not good. Saturday
didn't appear to be any better. My life looks a lot like either
one of them. Father, make me a Sunday person in a Friday/
Saturday world. Like your servant Paul, I want to know
you more, the power of your death and the miracle of
your resurrection. You have made us more than a "get by"
people. We are children of the King. Help us to live like it's
'in the morning'... today and every day. In Jesus. Amen.

Life Questions:

What is the difference between an 'Easter Bunny Easter' and a
'Resurrection Easter'? Who will show up first at your house in
the morning--- the big-eared furry friend (Easter Bunny) or
a Risen Christ? You don't have to have children to forget why
we celebrate the real reason for the season. Keep us focused
on you... we are a Passover people very much in the 'thick of
things'... We Love you. In Jesus. Amen.

Shane Stanford and Pokey Stanford

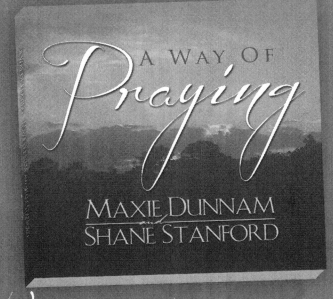

A WAY OF *Praying*

MAXIE DUNNAM
and
SHANE STANFORD

We do not believe that prayer should ever be reduced to a technique. Prayer is a relationship. It is communion with God. Our emphasis should never be on the mechanics of prayer. Even so, we must all find a way to pray. The plea of people from all walks of life is,

"I DON'T KNOW HOW TO PRAY;
CAN YOU HELP ME?"

This little book is a response to that plea.

It is a simple offering from us to you if that is your plea.

Available from Amazon.com

Getting to know us, getting to know all about us. . .

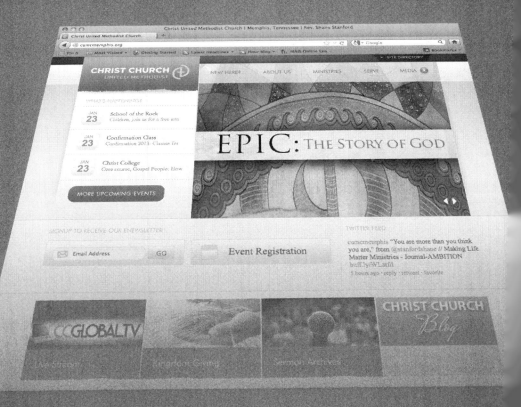

cumcmemphis.org

It's a good place to start.

Made in the USA
Charleston, SC
04 February 2013